THIS NOTEBOOK BELONGS TO:

Kleinberg Publishing

Enjoying this notebook?

Please leave a review on amazon because we would love to know your thoughts, feedback and opinions to create better paper products for you! Share how you creatively use your notebooks, journals, and stationery products.

Thank you so much for your support.

You are awesome!

Before you start...

Dear owner,

This notebook is your practical companion in everyday business life. It has been designed in co-operation with social workers and offers a variety of useful pages and tools to make your work in the company, in the team and the cooperation with your clients easier and clearer.

In this notebook you will find pages for notes for regular team meetings as well as for supervisions, lists of tasks that are often necessary in everyday life to prioritize, structure and check off, and pages for client documentation for client contact, be it during a home visit or to quickly write something down. At the end there are some useful tools.

We hope that you like this book and recommend it to others. Once again, we would like to remind you that we actively ask for feedback and/or customer reviews at www.amazon.de in order to be able to improve this product!

„When will finally the human being, the individual human being, precisely recognized in his necessities and individual possibilities, be the focus of consideration and not the structure of care?"

Arlt 1958: 31

TASKS	NOTES	STATUS
Call back miss X	not reached	

TASKS	NOTES	STATUS

| Miss Martina X. | 01.01.2020 |

Notes:

Happy

Unhappy

Other (decisions, new objectives, deadlines, specific perceptions, etc.)

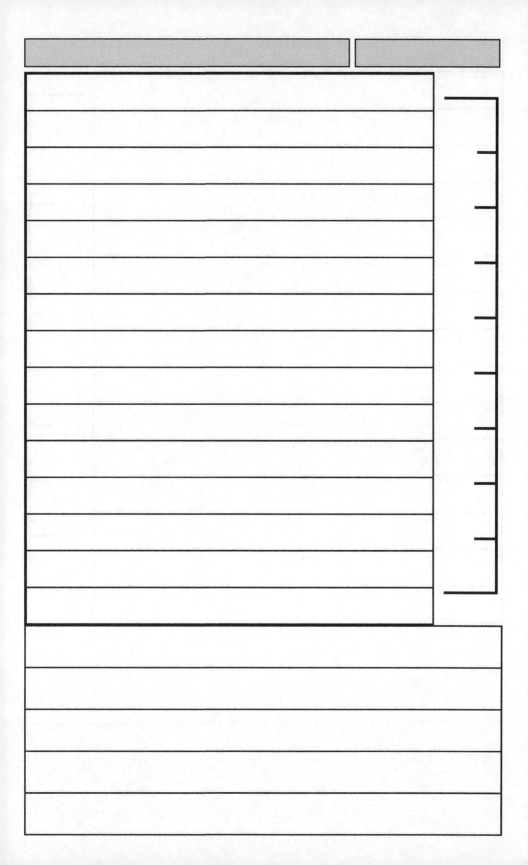

NOTES FOR THE TEAM MEETING

Date of the next team meeting: 31.01.2020

I need to keep minutes of my next team meeting.

Team decision on donations:

NOTES FOR THE SUPERVISION

Discuss challenging situation with Mr. Kleinberg and determine possibilities for action

NOTES FOR THE TEAM MEETING

NOTES FOR THE SUPERVISION

TASKS	NOTES	STATUS

NOTES FOR THE TEAM MEETING

NOTES FOR THE SUPERVISION

TASKS	NOTES	STATUS

NOTES FOR THE TEAM MEETING

NOTES FOR THE SUPERVISION

TASKS	NOTES	STATUS

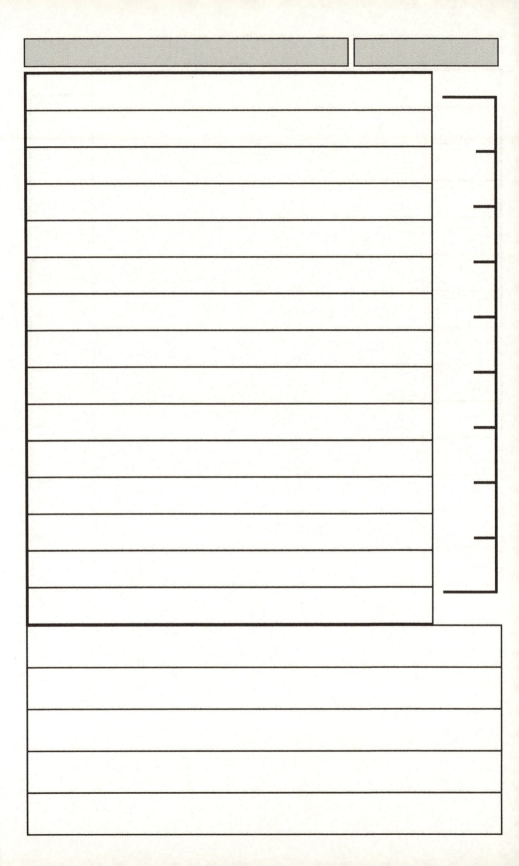

NOTES FOR THE TEAM MEETING

NOTES FOR THE SUPERVISION

TASKS	NOTES	STATUS

NOTES FOR THE TEAM MEETING

NOTES FOR THE SUPERVISION

TASKS	NOTES	STATUS

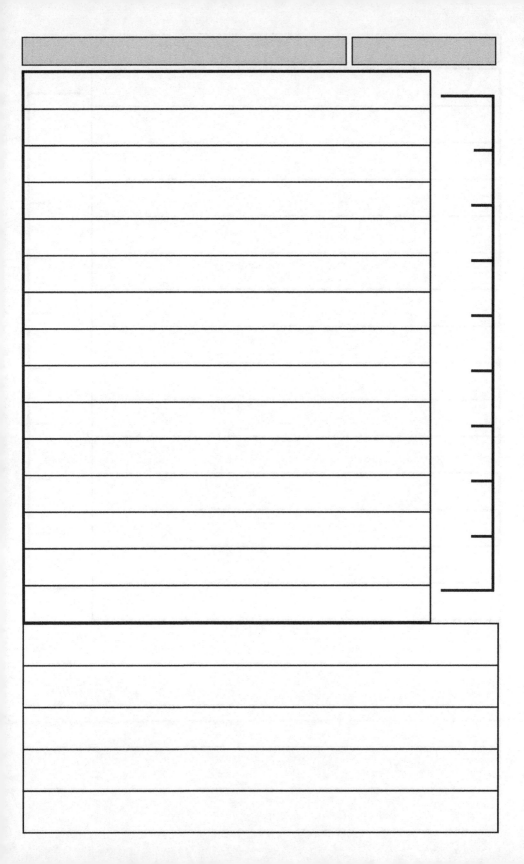

NOTES FOR THE TEAM MEETING

NOTES FOR THE SUPERVISION

TASKS	NOTES	STATUS

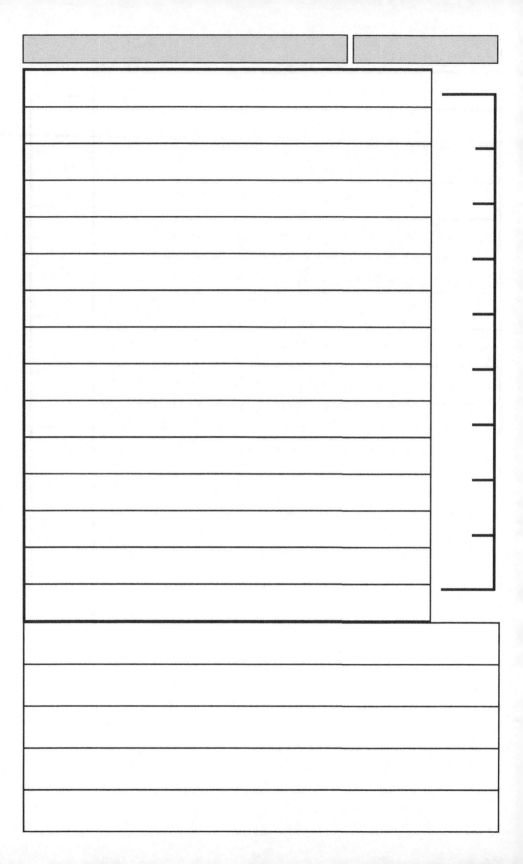

NOTES FOR THE TEAM MEETING

NOTES FOR THE SUPERVISION

TASKS	NOTES	STATUS

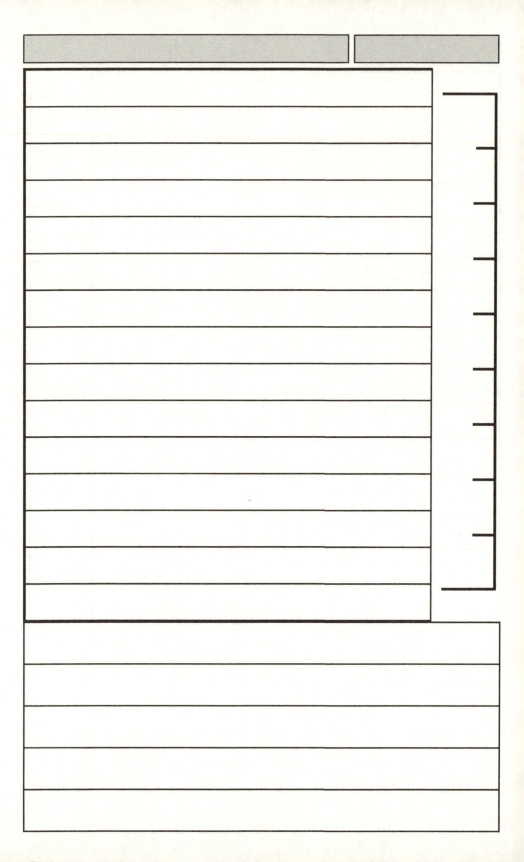

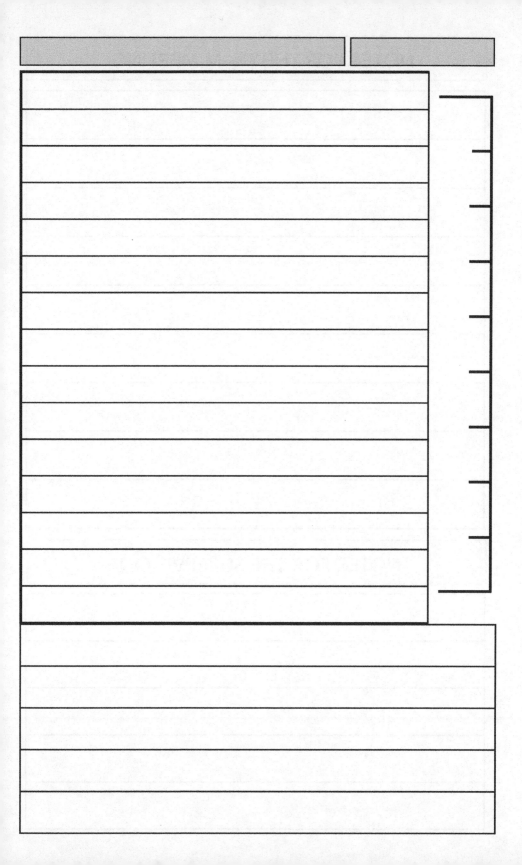

NOTES FOR THE TEAM MEETING

NOTES FOR THE SUPERVISION

TASKS	NOTES	STATUS

NOTES FOR THE TEAM MEETING

NOTES FOR THE SUPERVISION

TASKS	NOTES	STATUS

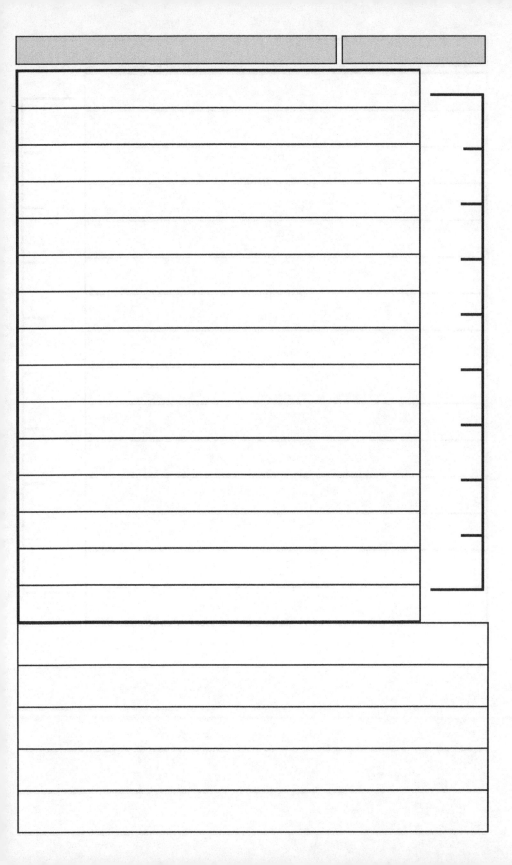

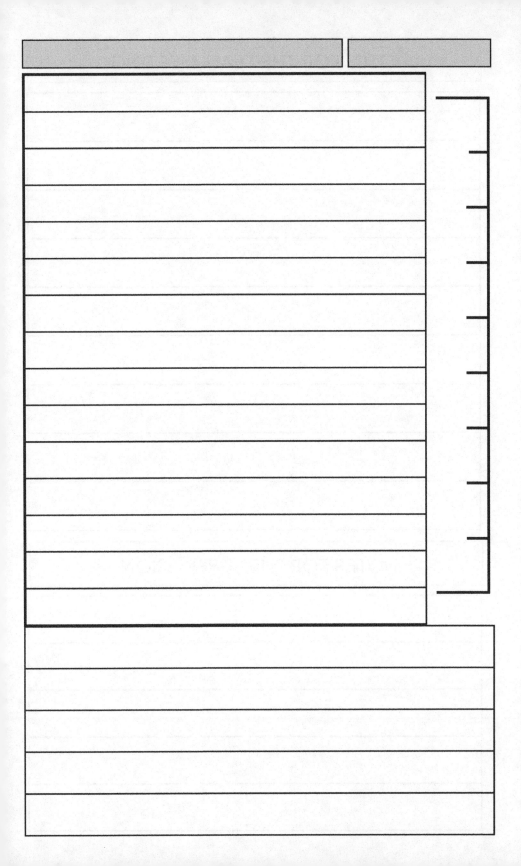

NOTES FOR THE TEAM MEETING

NOTES FOR THE SUPERVISION

TASKS	NOTES	STATUS

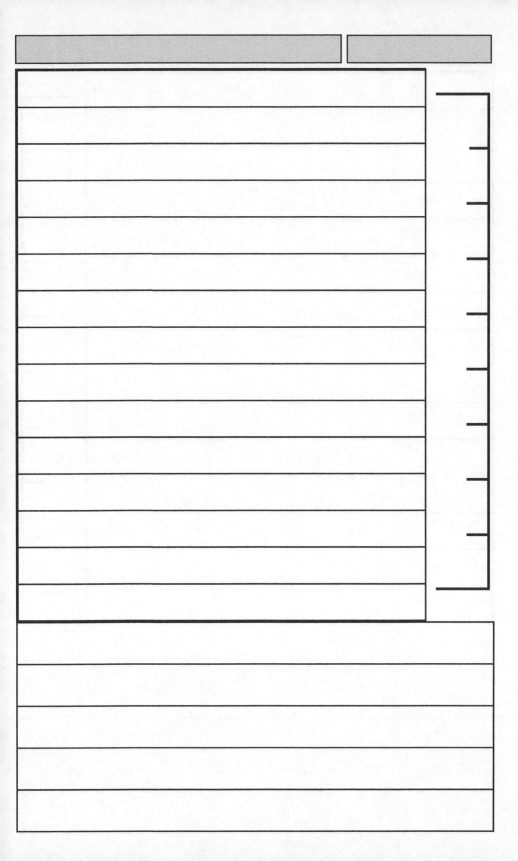

NOTES FOR THE TEAM MEETING

NOTES FOR THE SUPERVISION

TASKS	NOTES	STATUS

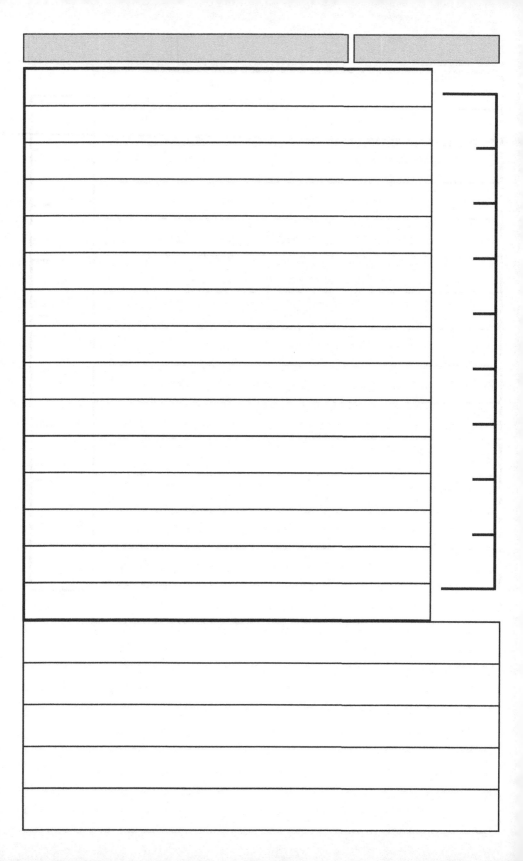

NOTES FOR THE TEAM MEETING

NOTES FOR THE SUPERVISION

TASKS	NOTES	STATUS

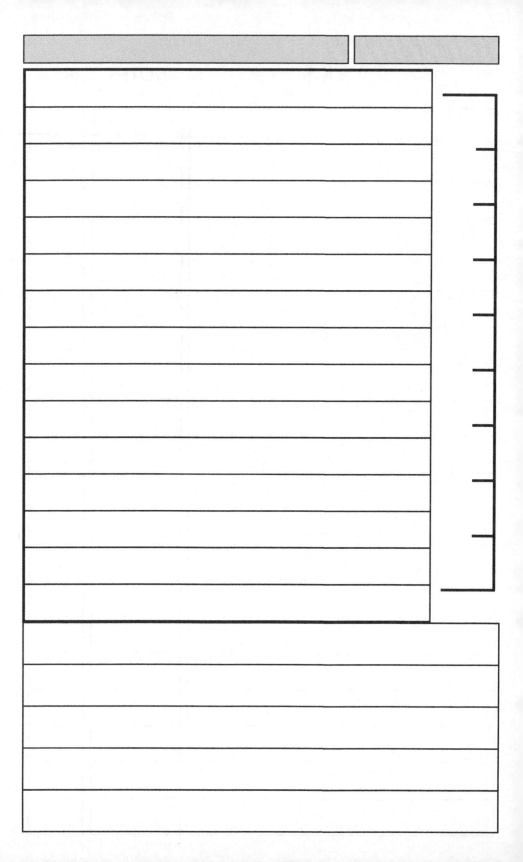

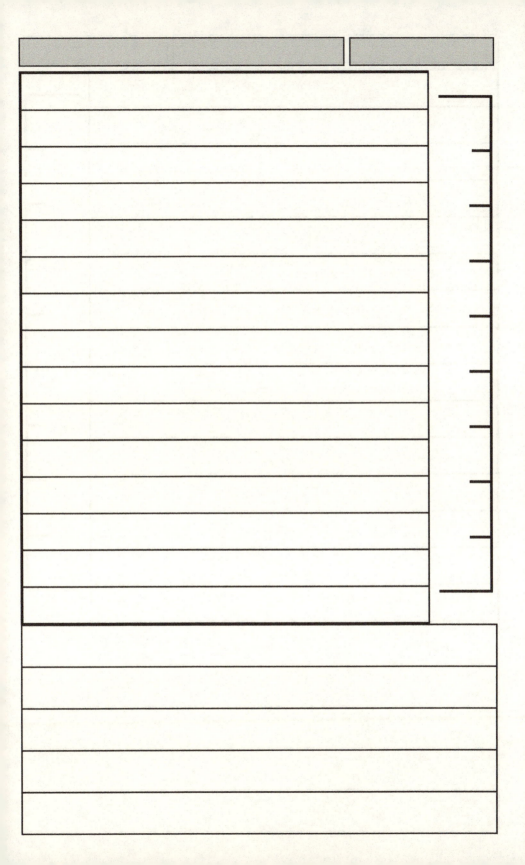

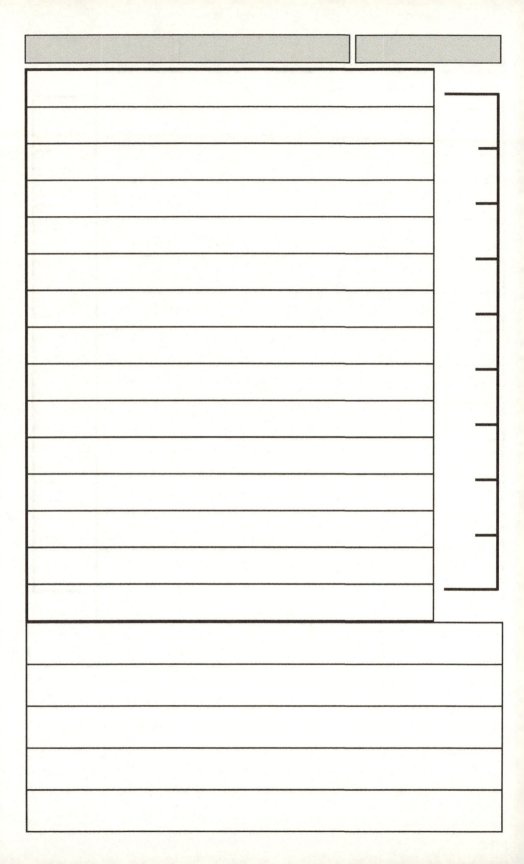

NOTES FOR THE TEAM MEETING

NOTES FOR THE SUPERVISION

TASKS	NOTES	STATUS

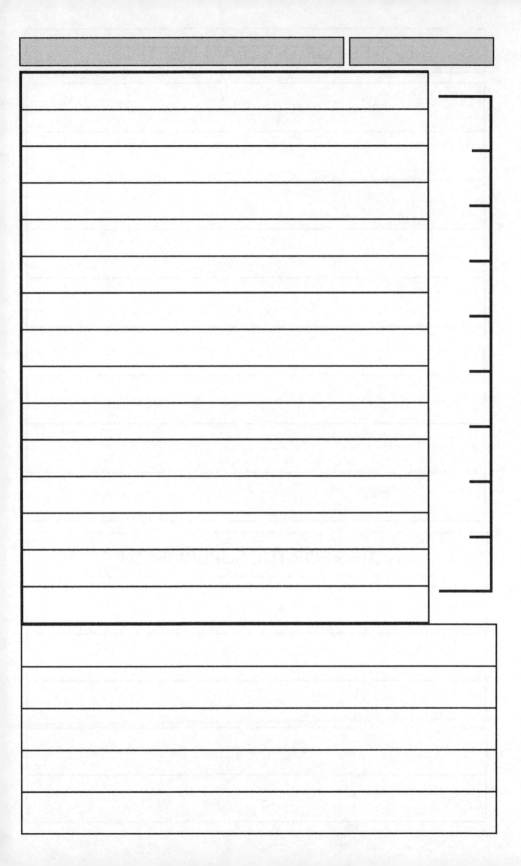

NOTES FOR THE TEAM MEETING

NOTES FOR THE SUPERVISION

TASKS	NOTES	STATUS

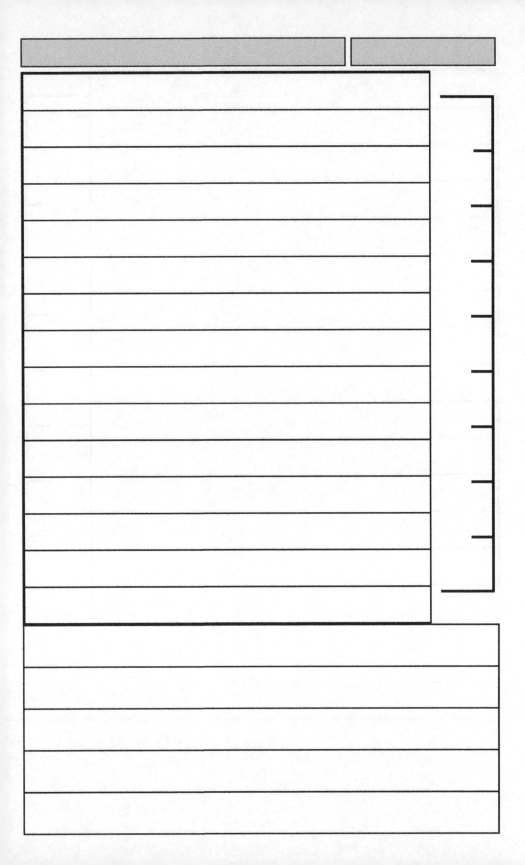

NOTES FOR THE TEAM MEETING

NOTES FOR THE SUPERVISION

TASKS	NOTES	STATUS

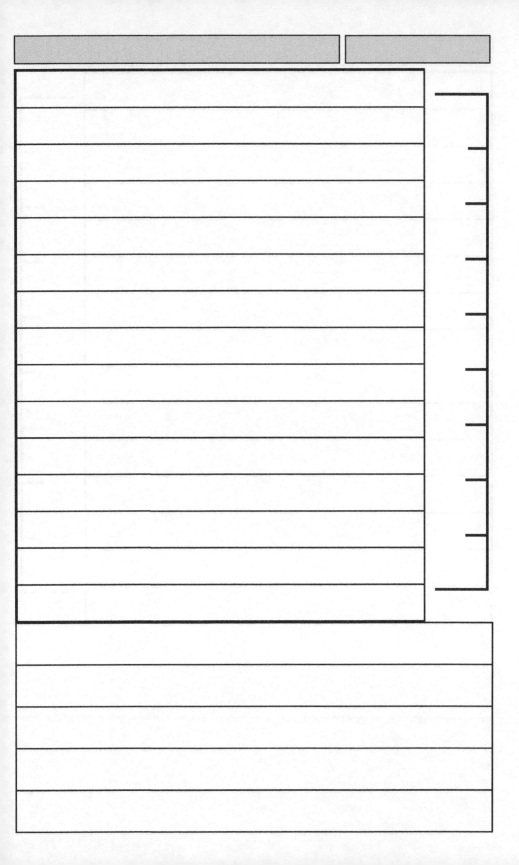

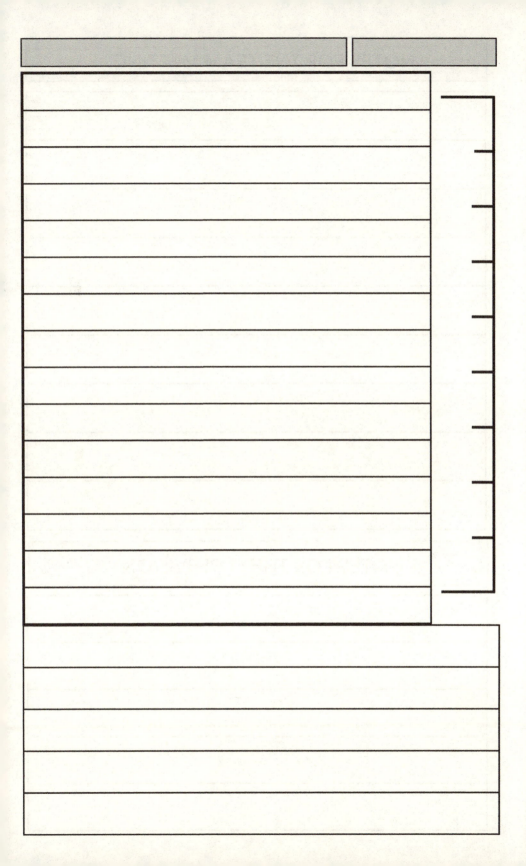

NOTES FOR THE TEAM MEETING

NOTES FOR THE SUPERVISION

TASKS	NOTES	STATUS

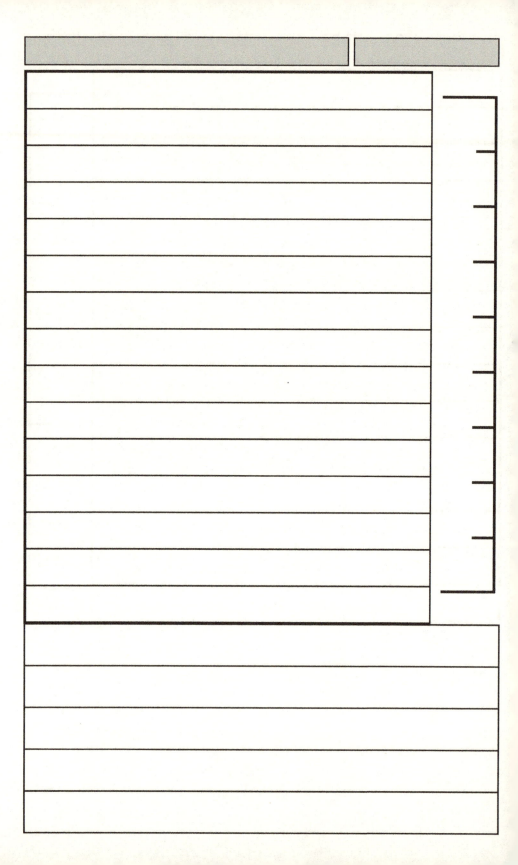

NOTES FOR THE TEAM MEETING

NOTES FOR THE SUPERVISION

TASKS	NOTES	STATUS

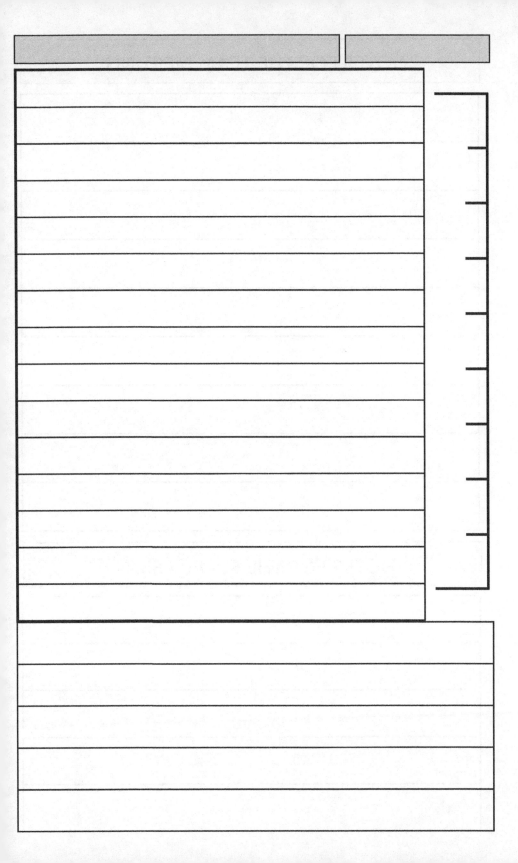

NOTES FOR THE TEAM MEETING

NOTES FOR THE SUPERVISION

TASKS	NOTES	STATUS

NOTES FOR THE TEAM MEETING

NOTES FOR THE SUPERVISION

TASKS	NOTES	STATUS

NOTES FOR THE TEAM MEETING

NOTES FOR THE SUPERVISION

TASKS	NOTES	STATUS

NOTES FOR THE TEAM MEETING

NOTES FOR THE SUPERVISION

TASKS	NOTES	STATUS

NOTES FOR THE TEAM MEETING

NOTES FOR THE SUPERVISION

TASKS	NOTES	STATUS

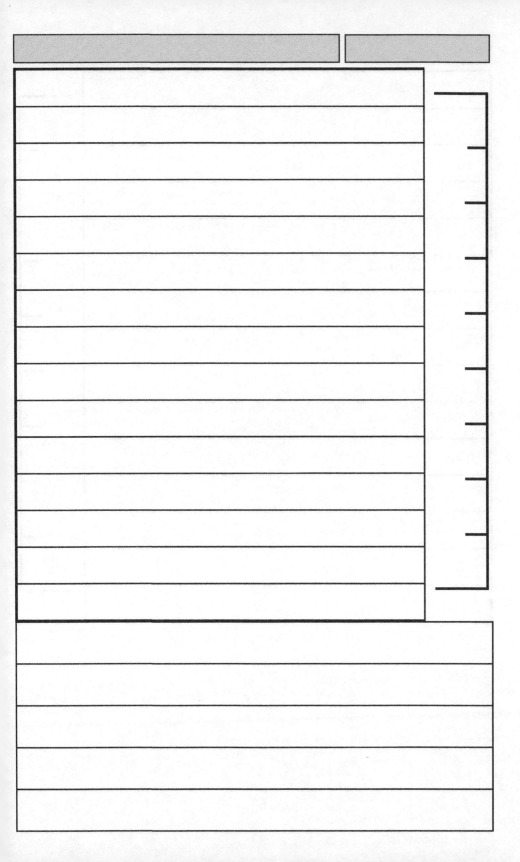

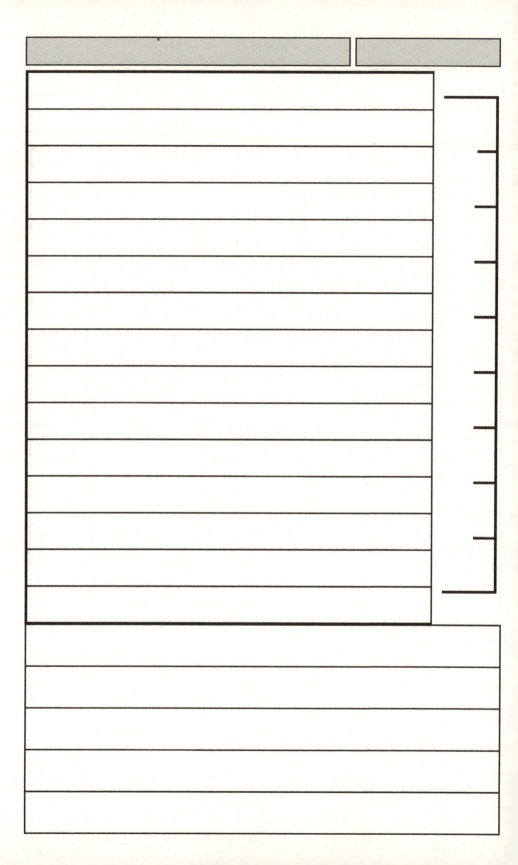

NOTES FOR THE TEAM MEETING

NOTES FOR THE SUPERVISION

TASKS	NOTES	STATUS

NOTES FOR THE TEAM MEETING

NOTES FOR THE SUPERVISION

TASKS	NOTES	STATUS

NOTES FOR THE TEAM MEETING

NOTES FOR THE SUPERVISION

TASKS	NOTES	STATUS

NOTES FOR THE TEAM MEETING

NOTES FOR THE SUPERVISION

TASKS	NOTES	STATUS

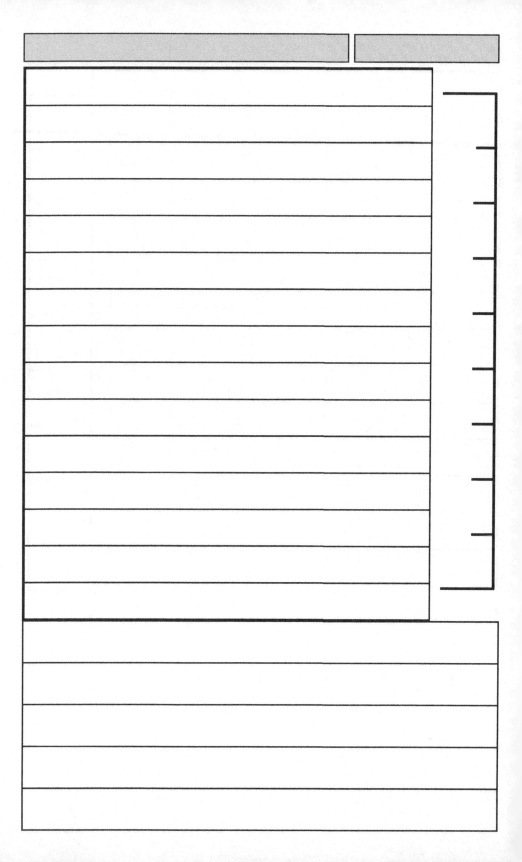

NOTES FOR THE TEAM MEETING

NOTES FOR THE SUPERVISION

TASKS	NOTES	STATUS

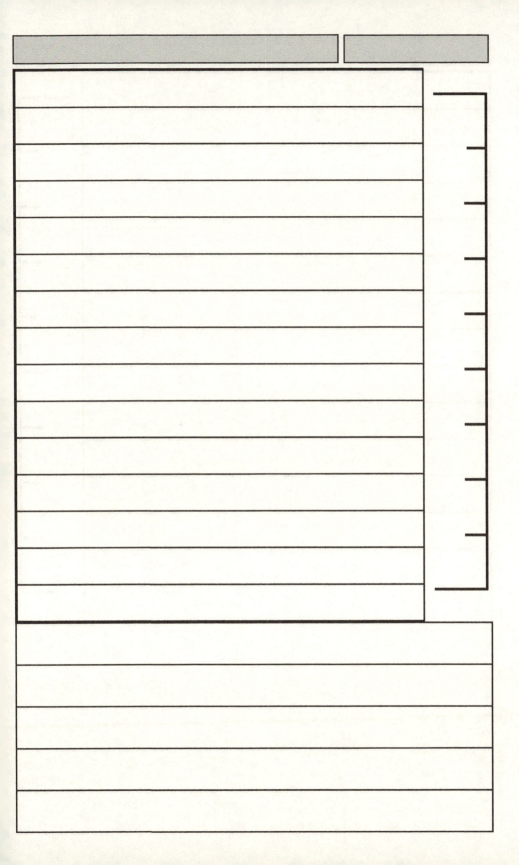

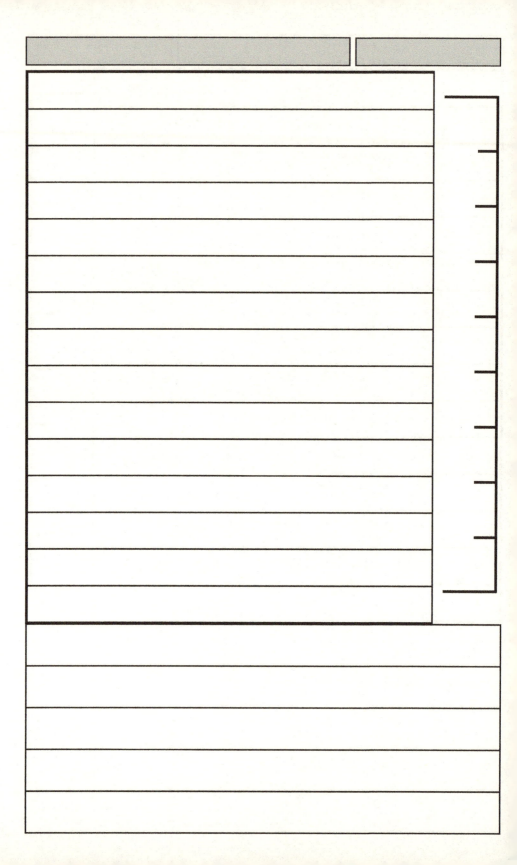

NOTES FOR THE TEAM MEETING

NOTES FOR THE SUPERVISION

TASKS	NOTES	STATUS

NOTES FOR THE TEAM MEETING

NOTES FOR THE SUPERVISION

TASKS	NOTES	STATUS

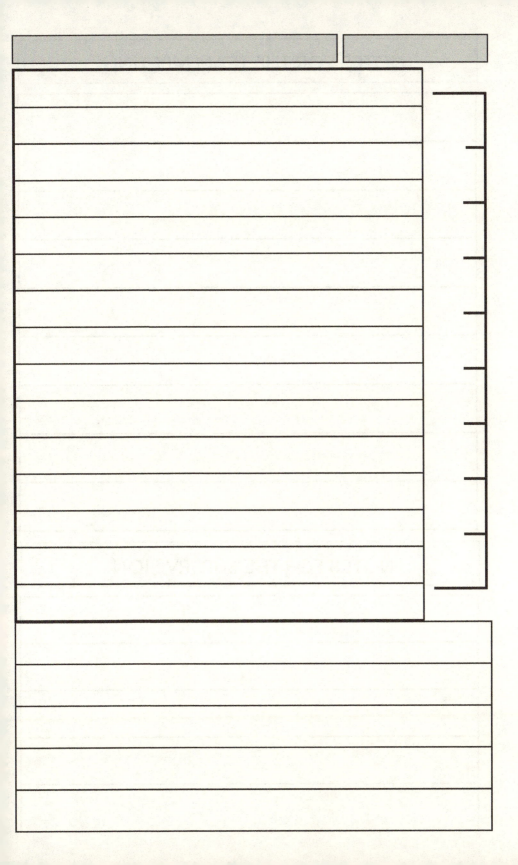

NOTES FOR THE TEAM MEETING

NOTES FOR THE SUPERVISION

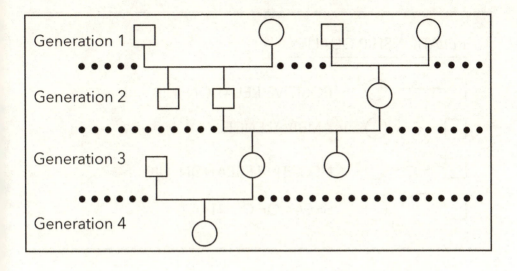

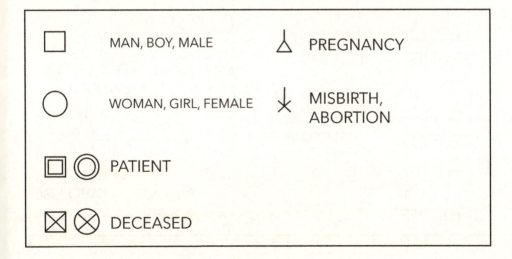

RELATIONSHIP QUALITY

□—+—○ POSITIVE RELATIONSHIP

□- - -○ AMBIVALENCE

□∿○ NEGATIVE RELATIONSHIP

□ ⁾ ○ BREAK OF CONTACT

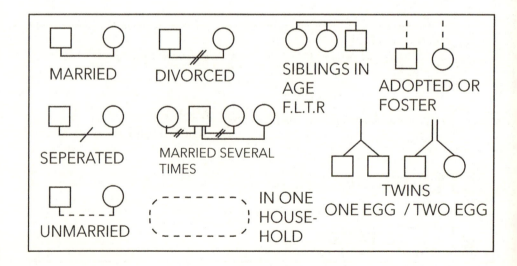

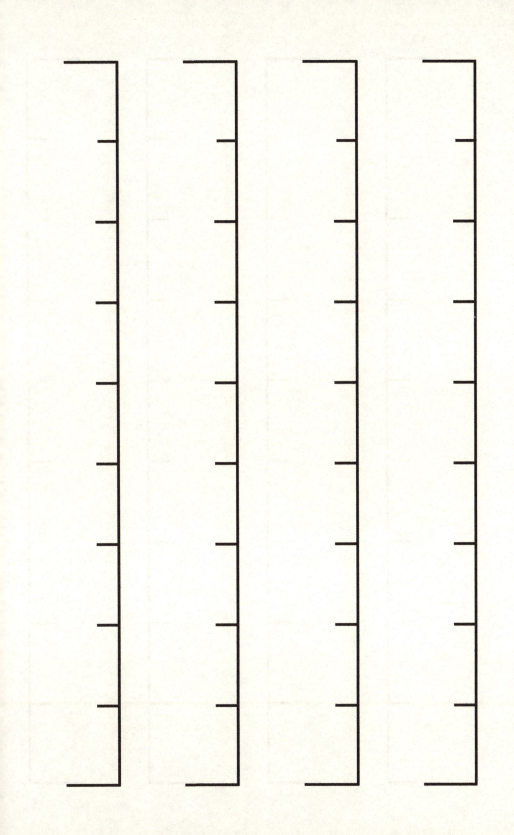

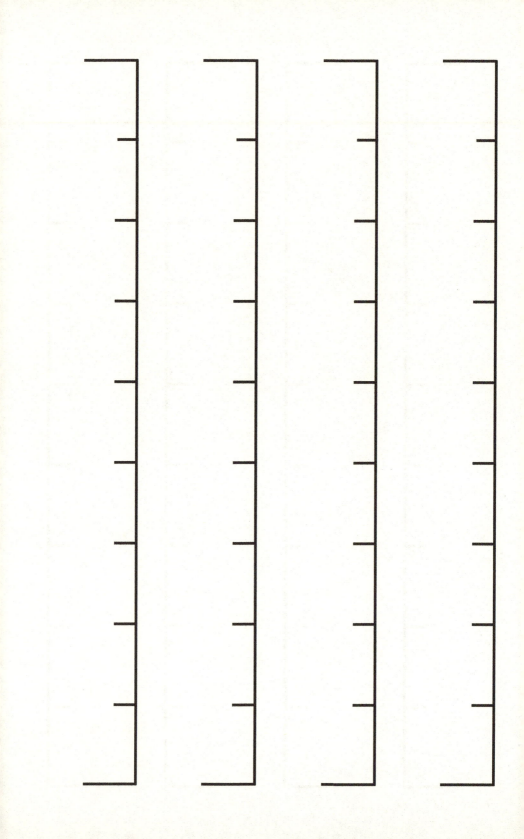

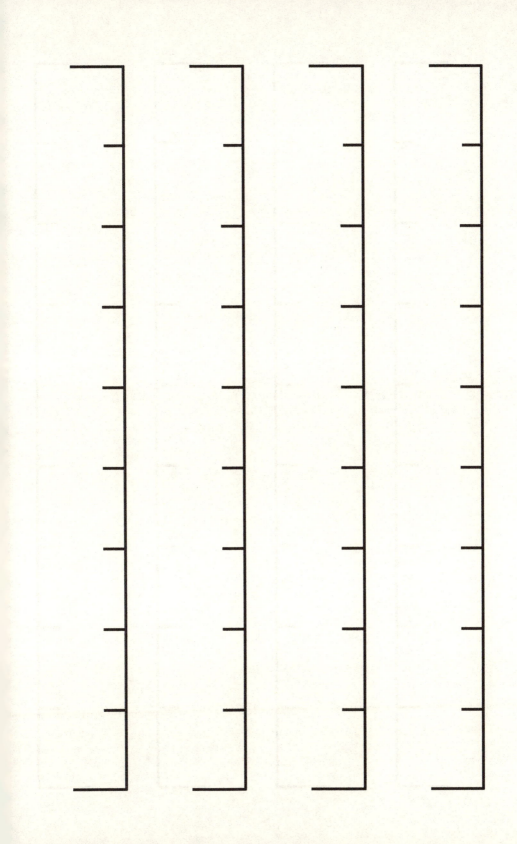

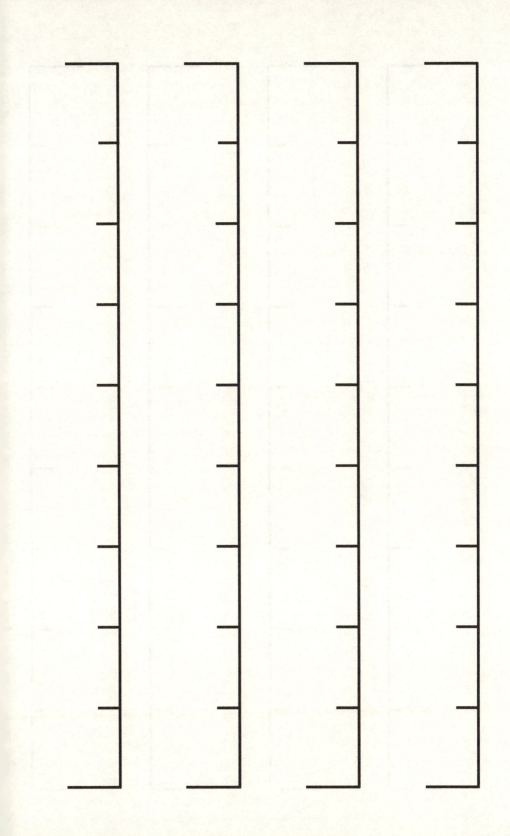

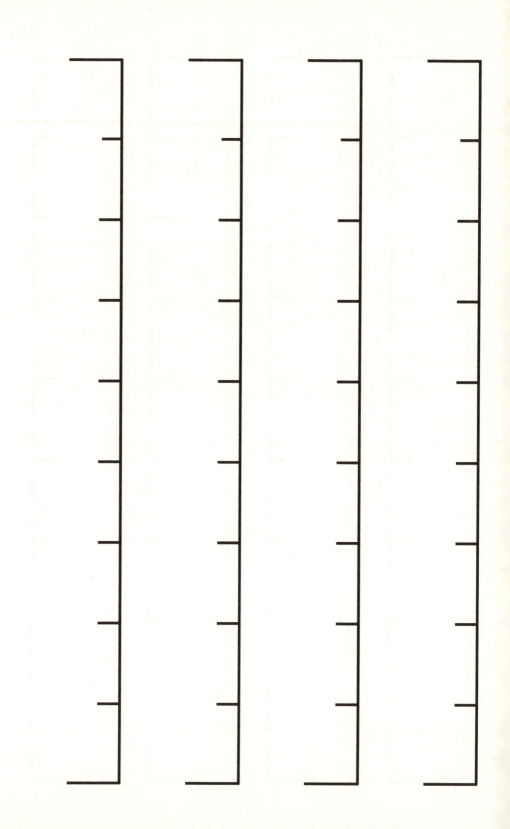

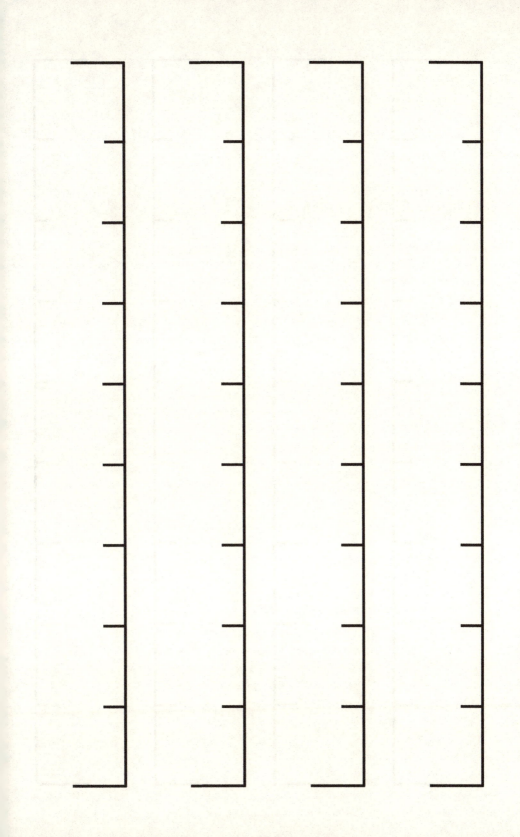

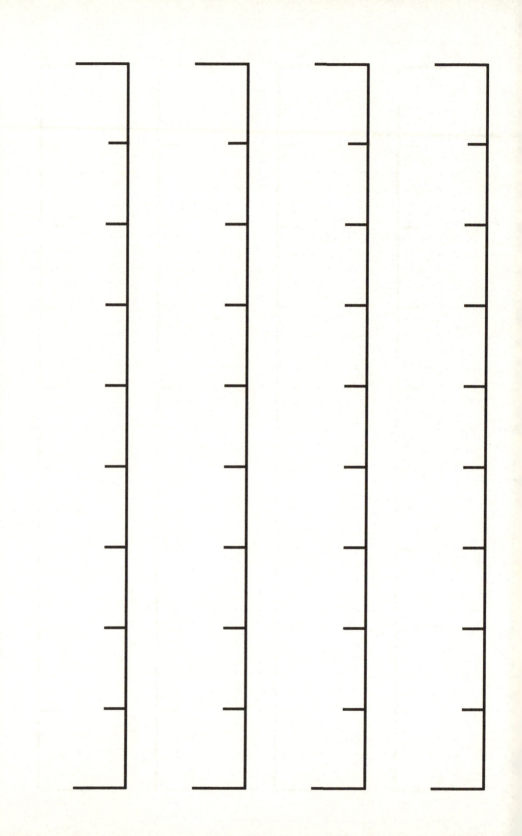

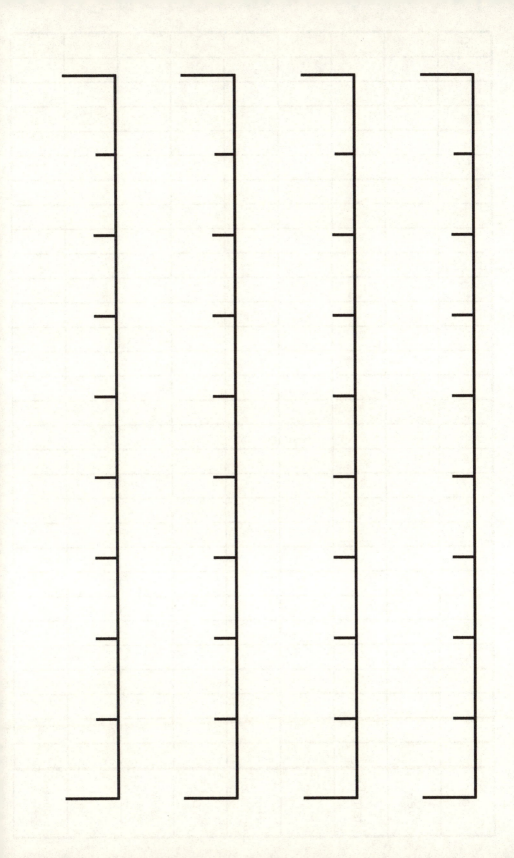

age	year	family	living	school / education	work	delin quency	health	treatment and help
5								
10								
15								
20								
25								
30								

age	year	family	living	school and education	work	Delinquency	health	treatment and help
35								
40								
45								
50								
55								
60								

age	year	family	living	school / education	work	delinquency	health	treatment and help
5								
10								
15								
20								
25								
30								

age	year	family	living	school and education	work	Delinquency	health	treatment and help
35								
40								
45								
50								
55								
60								

age	year	family	living	school / education	work	delin quency	health	treatment and help
5								
10								
15								
20								
25								
30								

age	year	family	living	school and education	work	Delinquency	health	treatment and help
35								
40								
45								
50								
55								
60								

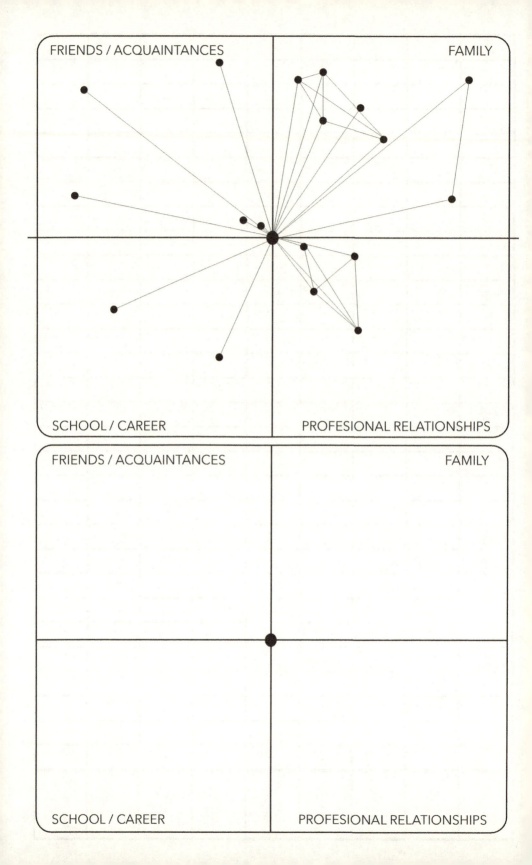

FRIENDS / ACQUAINTANCES	FAMILY
SCHOOL / CAREER	PROFESIONAL RELATIONSHIPS

FRIENDS / ACQUAINTANCES	FAMILY
SCHOOL / CAREER	PROFESIONAL RELATIONSHIPS

FRIENDS / ACQUAINTANCES	FAMILY
SCHOOL / CAREER	PROFESIONAL RELATIONSHIPS

FRIENDS / ACQUAINTANCES	FAMILY
SCHOOL / CAREER	PROFESIONAL RELATIONSHIPS

FRIENDS / ACQUAINTANCES	FAMILY
SCHOOL / CAREER	PROFESIONAL RELATIONSHIPS

FRIENDS / ACQUAINTANCES	FAMILY
SCHOOL / CAREER	PROFESIONAL RELATIONSHIPS

FRIENDS / ACQUAINTANCES	FAMILY
SCHOOL / CAREER	PROFESIONAL RELATIONSHIPS

FRIENDS / ACQUAINTANCES	FAMILY
SCHOOL / CAREER	PROFESIONAL RELATIONSHIPS

FRIENDS / ACQUAINTANCES	FAMILY
SCHOOL / CAREER	PROFESIONAL RELATIONSHIPS

FRIENDS / ACQUAINTANCES	FAMILY
SCHOOL / CAREER	PROFESIONAL RELATIONSHIPS

FRIENDS / ACQUAINTANCES	FAMILY
SCHOOL / CAREER	PROFESIONAL RELATIONSHIPS

FRIENDS / ACQUAINTANCES	FAMILY
SCHOOL / CAREER	PROFESIONAL RELATIONSHIPS

FRIENDS / ACQUAINTANCES	FAMILY
SCHOOL / CAREER	PROFESIONAL RELATIONSHIPS

FRIENDS / ACQUAINTANCES	FAMILY
SCHOOL / CAREER	PROFESIONAL RELATIONSHIPS

FRIENDS / ACQUAINTANCES	FAMILY
SCHOOL / CAREER	PROFESIONAL RELATIONSHIPS

FRIENDS / ACQUAINTANCES	FAMILY
SCHOOL / CAREER	PROFESIONAL RELATIONSHIPS

FRIENDS / ACQUAINTANCES	FAMILY
SCHOOL / CAREER	PROFESIONAL RELATIONSHIPS

FRIENDS / ACQUAINTANCES	FAMILY
SCHOOL / CAREER	PROFESIONAL RELATIONSHIPS

FRIENDS / ACQUAINTANCES	FAMILY
SCHOOL / CAREER	PROFESIONAL RELATIONSHIPS

FRIENDS / ACQUAINTANCES	FAMILY
SCHOOL / CAREER	PROFESIONAL RELATIONSHIPS

FRIENDS / ACQUAINTANCES	FAMILY
SCHOOL / CAREER	PROFESIONAL RELATIONSHIPS

FRIENDS / ACQUAINTANCES	FAMILY
SCHOOL / CAREER	PROFESIONAL RELATIONSHIPS

Copyright © 2020 Kleinberg Publishing
is represented by
Hämmerle Valentin
Kehlerstraße 25
6850 Dornbirn
AUSTRIA
Mail: haemmerle.valentin(at)gmx.at
all rights reserved

Made in United States
Orlando, FL
20 May 2024